Johann Sebastian Bach

Brandenburg Concertos Nos. 1–3

BWV 1046–1048

Edited by Karin Stöckl

Urtext

EULENBURG

Contents / Inhalt

EAS 102
ISBN 3-7957-6502-1
ISMN M-2002-2325-5
© 2006 Ernst Eulenburg & Co GmbH, Mainz
for Europe excluding the British Isles
Ernst Eulenburg Ltd, London
for all other countries
Urtext editions based on Eulenburg Study Scores ETP 280, 257 and 254
Preface by Ulrike Brenning taken from *Lexikon Orchestermusik Barock*, ed. Wulf Konold and Eva Reisinger,
© 1991 Schott Music, Mainz, SEM 8271, ISBN 3-7957-8271-6
CD ℗ & © 1999 Naxos Rights International Ltd

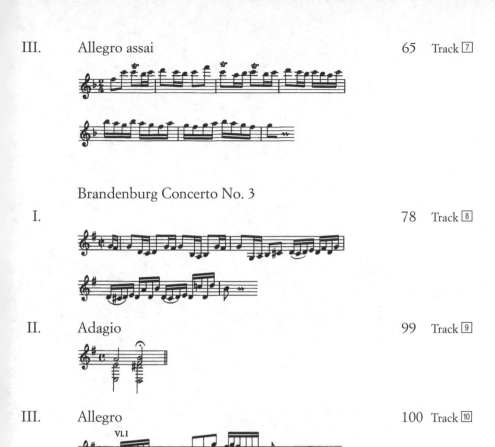

Preface

From August 1717 to April 1723 Johann Sebastian Bach was Kapellmeister and Master of the Royal Chamber Music at the Court of Prince Leopold of Anhalt-Cöthen. Bach expressed his feelings about this post retrospectively in a letter to his long-standing friend Georg Erdmann, written in 1730. One may gather from this letter that for Bach the well-paid post of Kapellmeister obviously carried with it a certain prestige and for that reason he felt it to be a demotion to have to trouble himself with a choirmaster's job. On the other hand Bach's comments make it clear that the working conditions in Cöthen became increasingly difficult with the approaching marriage of Leopold to Friederica Henrietta von Bernburg, which took place at the end of 1721. Bach had in fact, in November 1720, already tried to make a change by applying – though without success – for the vacant post of choirmaster at the Jakobikirche in Hamburg.

In this context the fact that Bach sent selected concertos to Berlin, in a dedicatory manuscript, beautifully prepared as a fair copy in his own hand, for Christian Ludwig, Margrave of Brandenburg, youngest son of the Electoral Prince, has particular significance. According to the requirements of his secular post, Bach composed almost exclusively keyboard works, chamber music and instrumental concertos during his time at Cöthen. So when he dedicates some of his works to an equally secular master it is natural to suppose that he would choose them from this repertory. Furthermore, in the text of the inscription (in French) to the Margrave dated 24 March 1721, he makes reference to concrete grounds for the dedication of these *Six Concerts avec plusieurs instruments*, named nowadays, after their dedicatee, the 'Brandenburg Concertos': 'A couple of years ago I had the good fortune to be heard by your majesty [...]. Your majesty honoured me with the request that I send you a few of my compositions.'

The circumstances of this performance have been much puzzled over. A coincidental meeting between Bach and the Margrave in Meiningen, of which Christian Ludwig's brother-in-law was Duke, or in Carlsbad during a trip made by Leopold early in 1718 would be possibilities; it is more likely however that Bach met the Margrave in Berlin at the beginning of 1719. Prince Leopold had ordered a harpsichord and instructed Bach to collect the instrument from Berlin – as can be verified from an item for travel expenses in the accounts for 1 March 1719.

The Margrave may well have expressed the desire to hear more of Bach's compositions at the time of this performance. The fact, however, that Bach did not comply with the Margrave's wishes until the sudden dedication of these six concertos two years later makes it much more likely that a secret request was the real reason behind the sending of the scores.

This theory is supported by further observations. As already mentioned, for the enclosures which accompanied this dedicatory manuscript Bach drew on the repertoire of instrumental concertos which he had in all probability composed in and for Cöthen – taking into account, of course, the circumstances in Berlin, with which he must have been familiar both from his journey there and from the lively exchange of musicians which took place between Cöthen and Berlin. He probably hoped to perform the concertos himself in Berlin.

In its six works the score mirrors the whole range of types of concertante ensemble music current at the time: the third and sixth concertos display the characteristics of social music-making most clearly, the second and fourth more the concerto grosso type, and Concertos 1 and 5 in their final autograph form document the development towards the solo concerto. Furthermore, a comparison with the copies, still in existence, of the early versions of Concertos 1, 2 and 3 made by the Bach scholar Christian Friedrich Penzel shortly after Bach's death in Leipzig, and of Concerto No. 5 made by Johann Christoph Altnickol, shows that the diversity of the concerto type was extended in many respects in the writing out of the dedicatory score. Bach enriched the instrumentation by the use of unusual instruments such as the *violino piccolo* in No. 1 and *flauto d'echo* in No. 4; he divided the cello part in No. 3 and expanded the cadenzas of the solo instruments in Concerto No. 5. In addition, the treatment of the sequence of movements shows Bach's desire to display his skills to the full – by choosing a two-movement composition for the third piece and by extending the first concerto in the drawing up of the manuscript to a quasi four-movement piece.

Although Bach provides a representative cross-section of his concertos in the dedicatory score, it would be mistaken to think of them in terms of a cycle. We have here merely a collection of pre-existing concertos composed as individual works.

After the death of Margrave Christian Ludwig the dedicatory manuscript came into possession of the Bach scholar Johann Philipp Kirnberger. He in turn handed the score on to his pupil Princess Amalie of Prussia and it was bequeathed with her library to the Joachimsthalschen Gymnasium. From there the score was finally passed on to the Berlin Staatsbibliothek. It was not published until 1850 when, on the centenary of Bach's death, the Brandenburg Concertos were printed for the first time by C. F. Peters in Leipzig.

Karin Stöckl
Translation: Penny Souster

Brandenburg Concerto No. 1
in F major BWV 1046

Composed: in 1718/1719
Original publication: unpublished during the composer's lifetime
Other versions: an earlier 3-movement version of this concerto survives
Instrumental ensemble: 2 horns, 3 oboes, bassoon, violino piccolo
[a smaller violin, tuned at higher pitch], violins I and II, viola, violoncello,
violone grosso, continuo
Duration: ca. 18 minutes

The strict alternating sequence of *tutti* and *concertino* passages in the first movement, [*Allegro*], is held together by the momentum of the main theme, which also provides a link between the short bursts of music on various groups of instruments. This main theme undergoes numerous changes throughout the movement – for example, in a shortened version, in the form of brief instrumental interjections, in a resetting in the minor key – until the original form is taken up again at the end of the movement (b 72). This main theme is used as the basis of the *concertino* sections, too; as these are taken through various polyphonic arrangements on different groups of instruments the resultant sound is quite distinct from that of the *tutti* sections, which tend to exploit the harmonic power of the main theme. The most marked contrast can be found between the *concertino* section in bb 48–72 and the final *tutti* section that follows it.

In the second movement, *Adagio*, the thematic detail of the first movement is replaced by an expansive melodic line in D minor. The first oboe and then the solo violin each present the entire theme, suggestions of which are then heard in the bass parts and continuo; above them, the two upper parts imitate one another closely, dovetailing together into one line that leads into a sighing theme (from b 29 onwards). After a last ornamented oboe entry the movement ends with a cadence into the dominant key of A major.

The main theme of the third movement, *Allegro*, reinforces the home key of F major with its chordal structure after this harmonic opening. The solo violin and the first oboe are often brought together in the *concertino* sections by making use of their complementary rhythms, with other parts joining them in similar fashion so that the movement is characterized by the sound of playful semiquaver sequences. Two unexpected *Adagio* bars (bb 82/83) check the momentum of the music before the reintroduction of the continuo line in bb 17–27 introduces the final section. Bars 95–103 transpose the corresponding bars from the beginning of the concerto (bb 27–36) from G major into C major, reaching the home key of F major again in the final *tutti* section from b 108 onwards.

In the fourth movement Bach makes a concession to the prevailing French influenced musical tastes of his time by including a dance form with two trios and even inserting a polonaise between them. This movement represents an unusual crossing over of forms, yet its elements are only superficially 'traditional'. Subtle technical details such as unusual phrase lengths (in the Minuet, 2x12 instead of 2x8 bars) introduce artificial irregularities, which mean that these dance movements are far removed from the commonplace.

Brandenburg Concerto No. 2
in F major BWV 1047

Composed: in 1719
Original publication: unpublished during the composer's lifetime
Instrumental ensemble: solo: trumpet in F, flauto (recorder), oboe, violin;
ripieno: violins I and II, viola, violone, violoncello and cembalo
Duration: ca. 10 minutes

For this concerto Bach chose an ensemble of woodwind instruments (oboe and recorder) with trumpet and violin – a unique instrumental combination for a concerto at that time. The sounds produced by this unusual solo quartet characterize the whole alternating sequence of *tutti* and *solo* sections throughout: a glance at the score is enough to show that the *solo* group has a decisive impact in every movement. This is particularly evident in the third movement, where the group of soloists clearly takes over the direction of the music, with the *ripieno* merely providing an accompaniment. The deliberate choice of an extreme tessitura – with the trumpet playing in the high *clarino* register, and the other solo instruments playing at the same elevated pitch – makes the *solo* sections even more aurally distinct from the *tutti* sections.

The relationship between the *solo* quartet and the quasi-choral *ripieno* accompaniment corresponds to the traditional *concerto grosso* form only very superficially. The instrumentation used here by Bach goes far beyond what was customary for this period and, together with the thematic development, helps to determine the musical structure. This is particularly apparent in the first movement, *Allegro*, where thematic fragments are continually repeated using different combinations of instruments. Not until all possibilities have been explored does Bach turn to a new aspect of the theme – a setting in the minor key, rearranging the theme contrapuntally and then leading both players and listeners quite unexpectedly back to the original form of the main theme (b 103). The suddenness of this transition is reinforced by the preceding cadence into A minor.

The second movement, *Andante*, inhabits a different sound world, as the trumpet is resting and the movement begins in the relative minor key of D minor. The sparse instrumentation contributes also to a completely different mood: the trio of soloists (recorder, oboe, violin) imitate one another throughout the movement, accompanied by the continuo. After a renewed entry in A minor (b 8 onwards) the theme moves into F major (b 15 onwards), introducing a brief moment of brightness. Sighing motifs derived from the theme then lead back to D minor. The movement ends with some unexpected dissonances, arising from a succession of seventh chords and diminished intervals.

The final movement, *Allegro assai*, is characterized by Bach's strict contrapuntal working through the succesive entries of each of the solo instruments. The trumpet begins, followed six bars later by the oboe in canon at a fourth below; after another six bars the canonic roles are reversed – the trumpet now imitates the oboe. The violin does not enter until b 21, followed six bars later by the first entry on the recorder a fifth above it. An imitative dialogue also develops between these two parts, before the trumpet takes up the theme in C major; only now does the *ripieno* play accompanying figures and short echoes of the opening theme. Both the opening and development sections of the movement are clearly led by the group of soloists, while the *ripieno* in the *tutti* passages have little thematic significance in the structure of the music beyond supplying the full harmony between the soloists and the basso continuo.

Brandenburg Concerto No. 3
in G major BWV 1048

Composed: in 1719
Original publication: unpublished during the composer's lifetime
Instrumental ensemble: violins I, II and III, violas I, II and III,
violoncellos I, II and III, violone and cembalo
Duration: ca. 11 minutes

With the instrumentation of this work Bach moved further away from the model of the *concerto grosso* than in any of the other five Brandenburg concertos: here each group of string instruments is divided into three different parts over a simple bass line, which often plays in parallel with the cellos. The purity of the string sound and the structure of the work as a *Gemeinschaftsspielmusik*, a convivial piece, brings it close in stylistic terms to the sixth Brandenburg Concerto, which was written at about the same time.

In the first movement, which has no tempo indication, the main theme emerges from ornamenting the notes of the G major chord G – B – D and the notes of this chord are then used as a basis for contrapuntal development (from b78); the rhythmic force of the main theme remains ever present, meanwhile, whether it is heard in unison in the *tutti* sections or shared between the solo parts. A sharp contrast is felt when this rhythmic stability gives way to two long sustained chords marked *Adagio*; then there is a sudden key change from the end of the first movement in G major to A major in the first inversion (with the bass parts having to leap an augmented fifth from G to C♯) and then B major. Since the first movement, the following *Adagio* and the third and final movement, *Allegro*, are not separated from one another with double bar-lines, it may be assumed that these movements are to be played continuously, without pauses, thus adding further to the harmonic tensions.

The third movement is likewise dominated by the rhythmic force of the main theme. Rippling chains of semiquavers accompanied by groups of quavers infuse the movement with a tempestuous flow. Once the theme has been introduced in all the parts, with entries half a bar apart, it remains audible almost all the time through the changing sounds of the quaver accompaniment.

After the first section, which is repeated and ends by moving into the dominant key, the main theme goes into the minor key in the second section, which is also repeated. Not until it has been thoroughly worked through in E minor, B minor and A minor does it move back to the home key towards the end of this section, with the piece ending on an arpeggio chord of G major.

Ulrike Brenning
Translation: Julia Rushworth

Vorwort

Vom August 1717 bis zum April 1723 war Johann Sebastian Bach am Hofe des Fürsten Leopold von Anhalt-Cöthen als Kapellmeister und Direktor der Fürstlichen Kammermusiken tätig. Über diese Anstellung in Köthen äußerte Bach sich rückblickend in einem Brief an seinen langjährigen Freund Georg Erdmann aus dem Jahre 1730, aus dem zu entnehmen ist, dass für Bach offenbar die gut dotierte Kapellmeisterstelle mit einem gewissen Ansehen verknüpft war und er es daher als Rückstufung empfand, sich um ein Kantorenamt bemühen zu müssen. Andererseits deuten Bachs Äußerungen darauf hin, dass die Arbeitsbedingungen in Köthen durch die bevorstehende Heirat Leopolds mit Friederica Henrietta von Bernburg, die Ende des Jahres 1721 erfolgte, zunehmend problematisch wurden, und tatsächlich hatte Bach sich bereits im November 1720 mit seiner – allerdings erfolglosen – Bewerbung um die vakante Kantorenstelle an St. Jakobi in Hamburg beruflich zu verändern versucht.

In diesem Zusammenhang erhält Bachs Übersendung von ausgesuchten Konzerten nach Berlin an den Markgrafen Christian Ludwig von Brandenburg, den jüngsten Sohn des Großen Kurfürsten, in einem von der Hand des Komponisten selbst in kalligraphischer Reinschrift verfertigten Widmungsautograph besondere Bedeutung. Den Obliegenheiten seiner weltlichen Anstellung gemäß komponierte Bach in der Köthener Zeit fast ausschließlich Klavierwerke, Kammermusik und Instrumentalkonzerte. Wenn er also einem ebenfalls weltlichen Herrn einige seiner Werke widmete, so ist es naheliegend, dass er sie aus diesem Repertoire auswählte. Im Widmungstext vom 24. März 1721 an den Markgraf (in französischer Sprache) bezieht sich Bach zudem auf einen konkreten Anlass für die Dedikation dieser *Six Concerts avec plusieurs instruments*, die nach ihrem Widmungsträger die heute geläufige Bezeichnung „Brandenburgische Konzerte" tragen: „Vor ein paar Jahren hatte ich das Glück, mich vor Ihrer Königlichen Hoheit hören zu lassen [...]. Eure Königliche Hoheit beliebte mich mit dem Auftrag zu ehren, Ihr einige meiner Kompositionen zu senden."

Über die Umstände des hier angesprochenen Vorspiels ist viel gerätselt worden. Eine zufällige Begegnung Bachs mit dem Markgrafen in Meiningen, dessen Herzog der Schwager Christian Ludwigs war, oder in Karlsbad anlässlich einer Reise Leopolds im Frühjahr 1718, wäre denkbar, wahrscheinlicher aber ist, dass Bach den Grafen direkt in Berlin Anfang des Jahres 1719 aufsuchte. Fürst Leopold nämlich hatte in Berlin einen Kielflügel bestellt und beordete Bach zur Abholung des Instrumentes dorthin, was der Posten der Reisespesen auf der Abrechnung vom 1. März 1719 belegt.

Wohl mag der Markgraf anlässlich dieses Vorspiels den Wunsch geäußert haben, von Bach weitere Kompositionen zu hören. Der Umstand jedoch, dass Bach erst nach zwei Jahren plötzlich mit der Dedikation dieser sechs Konzerte dem Wunsch des Markgrafen nachkam, deutet viel eher auf eine versteckte Bewerbung als wahren Grund für die Übersendung der Partitur hin.

Diese These lässt sich durch weitere Beobachtungen stützen: Wie bereits erwähnt, schöpfte Bach bei der Anlage seiner Widmungshandschrift aus seinem Repertoire von Instrumentalkonzerten, das er aller Wahrscheinlichkeit nach in und für Köthen komponiert hatte, wobei er natürlich die Berliner Verhältnisse berücksichtigt haben dürfte, die er aufgrund seiner Reise dorthin, aber auch aufgrund des regen Musikeraustausches, der zwischen Köthen und Berlin stattfand, genau gekannt haben muss. Er kann also durchaus gehofft haben, die Konzerte in Berlin selbst einmal aufzuführen.

Die Partitur spiegelt mit ihren sechs Werken die gesamte Palette damals gängiger Typen konzertanter Ensemblemusik: Das 3. und 6. Konzert prägen am ehesten den Charakter von Gemeinschaftsspielmusiken aus, das 2. und 4. mehr den Concerto-grosso-Typus und die Konzerte 1 und 5 dokumentieren in ihrer endgültigen Form im Autograph die Hinwendung zum Solokonzert. Darüber hinaus erweist ein Vergleich mit den noch vorhandenen Abschriften der Frühfassungen der Konzerte 1, 2 und 3 durch den Bach-Schüler Christian Friedrich Penzel, die dieser kurz nach Bachs Tod in Leipzig anfertigte, sowie des 5. Konzertes durch Johann Christoph Altnickol, dass die Vielgestaltigkeit der Konzert-Typen in mancher Hinsicht bei der Niederschrift der Widmungspartitur noch erweitert wurde. So bereicherte Bach die Besetzung durch die Verwendung ungebräuchlicher Instrumente wie des *Violino piccolo* im 1. und des *Flauto d'echo* im 4. Konzert, differenzierte den Cellopart im 3. und erweiterte die Kadenz des Soloinstrumentes im 5. Konzert. Außerdem zeigt die Behandlung der Satzfolge Bachs Intention, sein umfassendes Können zur Schau zu stellen, wenn er als drittes Stück eine zweisätzige Komposition auswählt und für die Erstellung des Autographs das 1. Konzert quasi zur Viersätzigkeit erweitert.

Obwohl Bach mit der Widmungspartitur die Darstellung eines repräsentativen Querschnittes durch sein Konzertschaffen gibt, wäre es verfehlt, von einem Zyklus zu sprechen: Es handelt sich lediglich um eine Sammlung präexistenter und als Einzelwerke komponierter Konzerte.

Das Widmungsautograph gelangte nach dem Tode des Markgrafen Christian Ludwig in den Besitz des Bach-Schülers Johann Philipp Kirnberger. Dieser wiederum übereignete die Partitur seiner Schülerin Prinzessin Amalie von Preußen, mit deren nachgelassener Bibliothek sie dem Joachimthalschen Gymnasium ausgehändigt wurde, von wo sie schließlich in den Besitz der Berliner Staatsbibliothek überging. Erst 1850, zu Bachs 100. Todestag, erschienen die „Brandenburgischen Konzerte" beim Verlag C. F. Peters in Leipzig erstmals im Druck.

Karin Stöckl

Brandenburgisches Konzert Nr. 1
F-Dur BWV 1046

Komponiert: 1718/1719
Originalverlag: zu Lebzeiten des Komponisten nicht gedruckt
Fassungen und Bearbeitungen:
Zu diesem Konzert gibt es eine ältere, lediglich dreisätzige Fassung.
Orchesterbesetzung: 2 Hörner, 3 Oboen, Fagott – Violino piccolo,
Violine I und II, Viola, Violoncello, Violone grosso, Continuo
Spieldauer: etwa 18 Minuten

Die strenge Tutti- und Concertino-Abfolge des ersten Satzes, *Allegro*, resultiert aus der bindenden Kraft des Hauptthemas: Es fasst die kurzzeitig konzertierenden Stimmengruppen immer wieder zusammen. Dabei ist es selbst vielen Veränderungen unterworfen: In verkürzter Gestalt, als knappe Zwischenrufe, in der Wendung nach Moll, erscheint es ständig anders, bis am Ende des Satzes (T. 72) die Anfangsform wieder aufgegriffen wird. Auch die Concertino-Abschnitte entwickeln sich aus dem Material des Hauptthemas; durch dessen differenzierte polyphone Verarbeitung in den Stimmengruppen entsteht die klangliche Abhebung gegenüber den Tuttiteilen, die das Hauptthema eher in seiner harmonischen Kraft nutzen. Am deutlichsten fällt die unterschiedliche Gestaltung im Concertino-Abschnitt T. 48–72 und dem hier eintretenden letzten Tuttiteil auf.

Die motivische Kleinarbeit des ersten Satzes wird im zweiten Satz, *Adagio*, durch eine weit ausholende melodische Linie in d-Moll ersetzt. Oboe I und nachfolgend die Solo-Violine führen sie jeweils vollständig vor, bis sie auch in den Bassstimmen und dem Continuo angedeutet wird; in den beiden Oberstimmen entsteht darüber eine dichte, einander imitierende Verzahnung dieser Linie, die in eine Seufzermotivik (T. 29ff) mündet. Der Satz endet nach einem letzten verzierten Oboeneinsatz in einer Kadenz zur Dominante A-Dur.

Das Hauptthema des dritten Satzes, *Allegro*, bekräftigt nach dieser harmonischen Öffnung in seinem dreiklangbetonten Aufbau wiederum die Grundtonart F-Dur. Solo-Violine und Oboe I werden in den konzertierenden Teilen oft unter Ausnutzung der komplementärrhythmischen, d. h. der einander ergänzenden rhythmischen Werte, kombiniert, andere Stimmen treten in ähnlicher Weise hinzu, sodass der Satz durch das Klangbild einer spielerischen Sechzehntel-Folge bestimmt wird. Zwei unerwartete *Adagio*-Takte (T. 82/83) stauen diese Bewegung, bevor unter Wiederaufnahme der Continuo-Linie in den Takten 17–27 der Schlussteil eingeleitet wird. Die Takte 95–103 transponieren die entsprechenden Takte des Anfangs (T. 27–36) von G-Dur nach C-Dur, die Grundtonart F-Dur ist im letzten Tuttiabschnitt ab T. 108ff wieder erreicht.

Im vierten Satz macht Bach ein Zugeständnis an den Zeitgeschmack, indem er eine Tanzform integriert und diese darüber hinaus mit zwei Trios versieht, zwischen die auch noch eine *Polacca* geschoben wird. Dieser Satz, in seiner formalen Verschränkung schon ungewöhnlich, bleibt jedoch nur an der Oberfläche „volkstümlich". Subtile technische Details wie beispielsweise ungewöhnliche Periodenbildungen (im *Menuetto* 2x12 statt 2x8 Takte) sorgen für artifizielle Unregelmäßigkeiten, die diese Tanzsätze dann doch weit vom Konventionellen entfernen.

Brandenburgisches Konzert Nr. 2
F-Dur BWV 1047

Komponiert: 1719
Originalverlag: zu Lebzeiten des Komponisten nicht gedruckt
Orchesterbesetzung: Soli: Blockflöte, Oboe – Trompete in F – Violine;
Orchester: Violine I und II, Viola, Violone, Violoncello und Cembalo
Spieldauer: etwa 10 Minuten

Mit der Besetzung dieses Konzertes führte Bach eine zur damaligen Zeit völlig unbekannte Kopplung von Holzbläsern (Oboe, Blockflöte) mit Trompete und Violine ein. Die Klangmöglichkeiten dieses ungewöhnlichen Solistenquartetts bestimmen denn auch das Wechselspiel von Tutti- und Soloabschnitten: Bereits aus dem Partiturbild ist zu ersehen, dass hier eine Gruppe von vier Solisten die Sätze entscheidend prägt (besonders deutlich im dritten Satz, wo die Solistengruppe eindeutig die Führung übernimmt, das Orchester lediglich begleitet); die Trompete in ihrer hohen Clarin-Lage und die dieser Höhe angepassten übrigen Soloinstrumente heben zusätzlich durch ihre hohe Klangfarbe die Soloteile von den Tuttiteilen ab.

Die Beziehung zwischen dem Quartett der Solospieler und dem chorisch besetzten Streichorchester stimmt also lediglich in der äußeren Form mit dem traditionellen Concerto grosso überein. Die Mittel der Instrumentation, die Bach hier verwendet, gehen weit über das damals Übliche hinaus und sind zudem neben der thematischen Verarbeitung Struktur bildend. Im ersten Satz, *Allegro*, wird das besonders deutlich, wenn Motivteile in ständiger Wiederholung, jedoch immer in anderen Instrumentenkombinationen auftreten. Erst wenn alle Möglichkeiten ausgelotet sind, wendet sich Bach einem neuen Motivteil zu, wendet das Thema nach Moll, kontrapunktiert die Motivteile und führt Hörer und Spieler sehr unerwartet aus den Klangexperimenten zurück zur ursprünglichen Form des Hauptthemas (T. 103).

Die Unvermitteltheit des Übergangs wird zusätzlich durch die vorangegangene Kadenz nach a-Moll verstärkt.

Im zweiten Satz, *Andante*, wird der helle Klang verlassen, indem die Trompete schweigt und der Satz zunächst in der parallelen Molltonart d-Moll beginnt. Auch die Sparsamkeit in der übrigen Instrumentation trägt zu einem völlig veränderten Charakter bei: Der Satz verläuft im einander imitierenden Solistentrio (Flöte, Oboe, Violine), lediglich gestützt vom Basso continuo. Nach einem erneuten Anlauf in a-Moll (T. 8ff) wendet sich das Thema nach F-Dur (T. 15ff), was eine kurzzeitige Aufhellung bewirkt. Seufzermotive, abgeleitet aus dem Thema, führen zurück nach d-Moll. Der Satz endet in eigenwilligen Dissonanzbildungen, die durch eine Aneinanderreihung von Sept- und verminderten Akkorden entstehen.

Der dritte Satz, *Allegro assai*, ist geprägt von der strengen kontrapunktischen Arbeit, mit der Bach das Spiel der Solostimmen gestaltet hat: Die Trompete beginnt, ihr folgt nach sechs Takten im Kanon in der Unterquarte die Oboe, wiederum nach sechs Takten wechselt die Führung im Kanon – es ist jetzt die Trompete, die die Oboe imitiert. Die Violine führt erst in T. 21 das Thema ein, nach sechs Takten gefolgt vom ersten Einsatz der Flöte in der Oberquinte. Auch zwischen diesen beiden Stimmen entfaltet sich zunächst ein imitierender Dialog, bevor die Trompete das Thema in C-Dur aufnimmt. Erst jetzt werden vom Orchester Begleitfiguren und kurze, aus dem Kopfthema abgeleitete Einwürfe gespielt: Der Beginn und die Entwicklung des Satzes gehen eindeutig von der Gruppe der Solostimmen aus, die Tuttipassagen sind ihres gliedernden thematischen Gewichts enthoben.

Brandenburgisches Konzert Nr. 3
G-Dur BWV 1048

Komponiert: 1719
Originalverlag: zu Lebzeiten des Komponisten nicht gedruckt
Orchesterbesetzung: Violine I, II und III, Viola I, II und III,
Violoncello I, II und III, Violone und Cembalo
Spieldauer: etwa 11 Minuten

Bach hat sich in der Besetzung dieses Werkes vom Concerto grosso so weit entfernt wie in keinem der anderen fünf Konzerte: die Streichergruppen zu je drei Stimmen, die ein schlichtes Bassfundament (häufig parallel zu den Celli) stützt. Der reine Streicherklang sowie der Aufbau des Stückes als eine „Gemeinschaftsspielmusik" rückt es stilistisch in die Nähe des sechsten Konzertes, mit dem es auch fast zeitgleich entstanden ist.

Im ersten Satz, der keine Tempovorschrift hat, bestimmen das Hauptthema, das auf der Umspielung der G-Dur-Dreiklangstöne g-h-d beruht, und der aus diesem Dreiklang gebildete Kontrapunkt (ab T. 78) die motivische Arbeit; dabei bleibt die Kraft des prägnanten Rhythmus des Hauptthemas immer erhalten, sowohl in der gleichzeitigen Ausführung in den Tuttiabschnitten als auch in der einander ergänzenden Verteilung auf die einzelnen Stimmen. Um so gegensätzlicher wirkt, dass auf die rhythmische Stabilität zwei lang ausgehaltene Akkorde folgen, die mit *Adagio* überschrieben sind, und auch der Wechsel der Tonarten ist unvermittelt: Auf den Schluss des ersten Satzes in G-Dur folgen A-Dur in Terzlage (wozu die Bassstimmen einen Tritonussprung g-cis ausführen müssen) und H-Dur. Da der erste Satz, das nachfolgende *Adagio* und der abschließende dritte Satz, *Allegro*, nicht durch fett geschriebene Schlussdoppelstriche voneinander getrennt sind, ist davon auszugehen, dass die Sätze ohne Unterbrechung ineinander übergehend vorgetragen werden sollen, dies erhöht zusätzlich die spannungsreiche Harmonik.

Auch im dritten Satz dominiert die rhythmische Kraft des Hauptthemas. Es sind die rauschenden Sechzehntel-Ketten, gestützt von Achtel-Gruppen, die den Satz mit einem stürmischen Bewegungsfluss durchziehen. Nachdem das Thema in halbtaktigem Abstand in allen Stimmen eingeführt wurde, ist es in Abwechslung und Begleitung der Achtel-Gruppen nahezu ständig präsent.

Nach dem ersten Teil, der wiederholt wird und sich am Ende zur Dominante öffnet, wendet sich das Hauptthema im zweiten, ebenfalls zu wiederholenden Teil, nach Moll. Erst nach ausführlicher Verarbeitung in e-Moll, h-Moll und a-Moll findet es gegen Ende dieses Teiles zurück zur Grundtonart; das Stück endet in einem arpeggierten G-Dur-Akkord.

Ulrike Brenning

Concerto No. 1

Johann Sebastian Bach
(1685–1750)
BWV 1046

I.

2

13

15

18

20

III. Allegro

24

28

IV. Menuet

Trio 1

Menuet da Capo
e poi la Poloinesse

Poloinesse

Menuet da Capo
e poi il Trio II

Trio 2

Corno (F)

Tutte le
Oboi

Menuet da Capo
al Fine

Appendix
Trio pour les Cors de chasse

Menuet da Capo
al Fine

Concerto No. 2

Johann Sebastian Bach
(1685–1750)
BWV 1047

© 2006 Ernst Eulenburg Ltd, London
and Ernst Eulenburg & Co GmbH, Mainz

58

tasto solo

accomp.

II. **Andante**

III. Allegro assai

Concerto No. 3

Johann Sebastian Bach
(1685–1750)
BWV 1048

84

II. **Adagio**

III. Allegro

Vl.

Vle.

Vc.

V. e C.

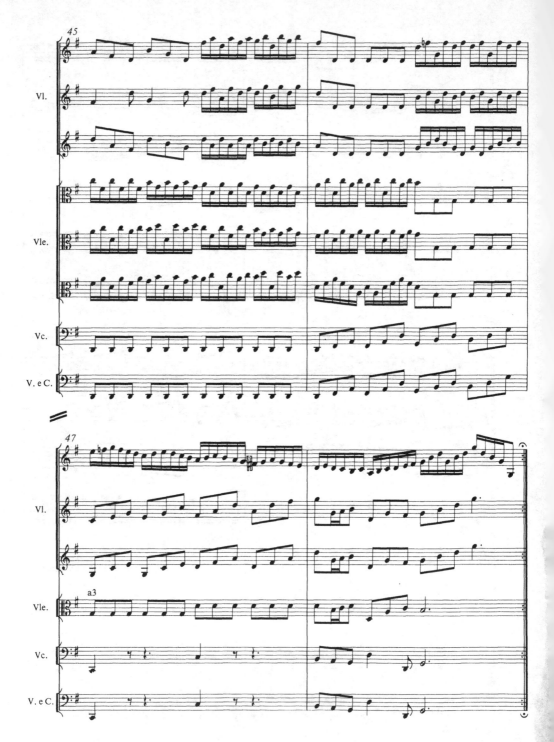

Printed in China